THE ULTIMATE PERSON

BY
CARMEN
TRIPODI

ISBN 978-1-7326977-2-0

Published By:

UltimatePerson.com LLC
P.O. Box 11973
Zephyr Cove, NV 89448

CONTENTS

INTRODUCTION

Everyone wants to have the best life and be the best person. It is as if these values are built into the human genetic code. The problem is that, up until now, there has been no accurate and reliable definition of the best life and the best person. Without such an accurate and reliable definition, people just flounder around using trial and error, not knowing if they succeeded or not.

This book provides the accurate and reliable definition of the best life and best person. Now that people have an accurate definition of the best life and the best person, they can take the steps to actually have the best life and be the best person. Everyone can now easily have the best life and be the best person, and get all the tremendous benefits. Regardless of their current status in life – rich or poor, popular or unpopular, happy or un-happy – anyone can now easily become a best person and have the best life.

This book defines best life and best person in terms of an ultimate life and an ultimate person, and they are defined scientifically. This "ultimate scientific" approach has two major advantages. First of all, the word "ultimate" is used and is defined as the "best of all time," not simply the best. So "best life" and "best person" are defined as "best life of all time" and "best person of all time." Secondly, the scientific method is used to ensure scientific validity which ensures accuracy and reliability in the definitions. The net result is accurate and reliable definitions of the best life of all time and the best person of all time.

The underlying science is an advanced topic and is explained in a companion book entitled *The Ultimate World*. This book entitled *The Ultimate Person* provides a basic introduction to the topic and defines the what, how, why and when of the ultimate person.

To start things off, here is a brief definition of what an ultimate person is. The first word "ultimate" is defined here to mean *best of all time*. The second word "person" is defined here in terms of *human behavior*. So the ultimate person is defined here in terms of the *best human behavior all of time*. What is the best human behavior of all time? Simply put, the best human behavior of all time is problem solving behavior. Problem solving is the best behavior because it leads directly to solutions to actual problems in the world. This includes the most serious problems in the world such as war, violence, poverty, disease, hunger, racism, and sexism.

The single most serious problem facing humans is the human survival problem. Despite all the problems we hear about in the news each day, there is no problem more serious than the human survival problem. This is because human extinction would be the most catastrophic event imaginable to humans. It would be the complete end of the human species. Here are four primary implications of human extinction:

1) an inconceivably large number of human lives would be lost by not being born;

2) the significance of the lives of all the billions of people alive today would be lost:

3) the significance of the lives of all the billions of our ancestors would be lost;

4) everything in history associated with being human, including all culture, all art, and all science would be lost.

Please take a minute and think about these implications. This is not your average news story.

So the human survival problem is the ultimate problem. It is explained in more detail in Chapter 3 entitled, *Why Everyone Needs To Be An Ultimate Person.*

Now, let's briefly explain the solution to all these serious human problems. The solution to all the world's problems, including the human survival problem, is simply for everyone to learn one new skill. Once everyone begins to learn this one new skill, all the world's problems will begin to be solved. What is this one new skill that everyone needs to learn? It is a problem solving skill officially called *maximum problem solving skill over time.* It is a skill that anyone can learn in a short period of time, so that the solution to all the serious problems in the world can be implemented in a time efficient manner.

This book is the textbook for the free online course that teaches the skill of *maximum problem solving skill over time.* The free course is available at www.ultimateperson.com. By teaching the skill of *maximum problem solving skill over time* around the world, this course serves as the simple solution to all the world's problems, and it implements this solution free of charge to the world.

Upon completion of the course, you will obtain a certificate that certifies you as an official Ultimate Person – see the sample certificate in Appendix D. It is an achievement that you can be proud of and will want to share with others. Sharing is simple, just refer people to www.ultimateperson.com. There, people can get a free copy of this book, and register for the free course. Sharing this free book and course means a lot more than just sharing your new outstanding achievement with your friends. It will actually help solve all the world's problems because you will be sharing the solution to all the world's problems.

Your first impression of all this may be that it sounds too good to be true. Well, it is all true because it all based on science. The science adds credibility to everything: to the definition of the ultimate person; to the process of becoming an ultimate person; and to the explanation for why ultimate person education is mandatory for everyone in the world. The science also adds credibility and value to your certificates. After completing the free course, you can say to your friends and associates – "I am certified ultimate person, backed by science," or you can simply say "I am a true ultimate person."

The science of the ultimate person adds credibility and value because it focuses on accuracy and reliability in the terminology. An advanced course on the science is also available at www.ultimateperson.com, for those who want to learn it and become an expert on ultimate living.

1

WHAT IS AN ULTIMATE PERSON?

     The Ultimate Person is defined in terms of human behavior. It is not defined in terms of an actual person, nor is it defined in terms of any physical attributes of humans. This focus on behavior has the advantage of being an objective, unbiased, action-based definition suitable for scientific inquiry.

     The first word of Ultimate Person, "ultimate," is defined here to mean the "best of all time." The second word "person" is defined in terms of human behavior. So the ultimate person is defined here in terms of the "best behavior of all time."

     Problem solving behavior is the best behavior of all time because it leads directly to solutions to actual human problems in the world. This includes the most serious human problems such as war, violence, poverty, racism, and sexism. Above all, it includes the solution to the most serious problem facing humans, namely, the human survival problem.

The Scientific Definition of The Ultimate Person

The Ultimate Person is scientifically defined as "a person who maximizes problem solving skill over time." The underlying science of this definition is an advanced topic and is given in a companion book entitled *The Ultimate World*. This companion book is centered around a new breakthrough scientific theory entitled Ultimate World Theory. The science of the Ultimate Person is defined within the context of Ultimate World Theory. An overview of Ultimate World Theory is given in Appendix A3 of this book.

The basic justification for *maximum problem solving skill over time* is that is necessary due to the maximum complexity of the human survival problem. For instance, surviving the universe is going to require colonizing space, which is an extremely complex problem. It is one of the most complex problem imaginable to humans. We can be certain that the complexity of the human survival problem, which is explained in detail in Chapter 3, is going to require maximum problem solving skill to over time solve it. This certainty about the need for maximum problem solving skill over time validates the central hypothesis of Ultimate World Theory (this exact hypothesis is given in Appendix A3). As Albert Einstein said when explaining his theory of relativity – "the theory is correct."

This book, *The Ultimate Person*, and the online course entitled Ultimate Person Course, focus on the skill of *maximum problem solving skill over time*, and putting it into practice on a daily basis.

Maximum problem solving skill over time (MPSSOT) is a problem solving skill that was developed as a way to solve problems of maximum complexity. It has five primary elements:

1) *Maximum clarity of problem and solution identification* – MPSSOT includes the skill of clearly identifying problems and solutions. All problems are identified in detail, and the solutions are defined in terms of the specific, doable, actions necessary to solve the problem.

2) *Maximum performance of the actions* – MPSSOT includes a process for maximizing performance (i.e. success) on the doable actions (i.e. the solution).

3) *Optimal emotional experience* – the action performance process is based on a scientific theory of optimal experience (also known as maximum happiness). The science shows us that maximum action performance and optimal emotional experience are directly linked. This way people will not only maximize their problem solving performance, but also maximize their individual happiness.

4) *Maximum improvement over time* – MPSSOT includes a built-in feedback mechanism so that feedback can be used to correct mistakes, adapt to change, improve performance, and improve problem solving skill, over time. MPSSOT is not a one-shot deal. It is an on-going experience in ultimate living.

5) *Direct relevance to the human survival problem* – All problems and solutions have built-in reasoning for relevance to the human survival problem. All problems, including both individual and group problems, are actually sub-problems of the human survival problem.

Although MPSSOT was developed as a way to solve problems of maximum complexity, it can be used to solve any problem. At its most simplified level, MPSSOT is just a super-innovative, high performance system of to-do lists, such as a grocery list. Everyone knows how to do a grocery list, right? This means anyone can learn and understand MPSSOT.

The Simple Solution To All The World's Problems

The solution to all the world's problems, including the most serious problems such as war, violence, poverty, racism, and sexism, is simply to have everyone learn one new skill. Once people begin to learn this new skill, all the world's problems will begin to be solved. And you guessed it, the skill that everyone needs to learn is *maximum problem solving skill over time.* Here is how it will work.

First of all, MPSSOT is a problem solving skill that applies to both groups and individuals. At the group level, MPSSOT solves problems by identifying group problems that all group members work together on as a problem solving team. Teamwork is encouraged by having each member of the group focus on a specific sub-problem of the group problem.

A classic example of a group problem solving team is the sports team – for example, a soccer team. The soccer team consists of forwards who focus on the sub-problem of scoring goals, defensemen who focus on the sub-problem of defense, and a goalie who focuses on the sub-problem of protecting the goal. Each member of the soccer team works together to solve the group problem of scoring more goals than their opponent. Conflict between team members is eliminated because each team member is applying all their energy on their specialized sub-problem, and enjoying the success of the group.

Business organizations, music bands, sports teams, and virtually any group of people apply group problem solving in the same way. The groups that are most successful are the ones who apply group problem solving most effectively.

The ultimate group problem solving scenario is for the entire world to work together as a team to solve the ultimate problem of the human survival of the universe. Everyone in the world would work on specific sub-problems of the human survival problem, and enjoy the success of the world in solving the human survival problem. The world would behave as a high performance problem solving team and all conflict between humans would be eliminated.

Many of the social problems in the world such as war, violence, racism and sexism are conflict related, and these conflict related problems would automatically be solved because the underlying conflict would be eliminated. Human survival is a common goal of all humans all around the world and we need to unite around this common goal.

At the individual level, MPSSOT solves problems by identifying individual problems that are actually sub-problems of the group problem of human survival. These sub-problems are essentially an individual's job or occupation. By assisting individuals in maximizing their individual problem solving skill, everyone maximizes their contribution to the group problem of human survival.

For example, doctors would be more productive in helping patients stay healthy. Drug researchers would be more productive in developing drugs to cure more diseases such as cancer. Scientists would be more productive in defining and testing theories related to the human survival problem. Businesses would be more productive in developing their products and services. Everyone in the world would be more productive, thereby increasing the productivity of the world exponentially. And all this productivity would be achieved at much lower costs.

MPSSOT also helps individuals in solving other personal issues such as health and financial issues by identifying specific problems and solutions (action lists), and maximizing performance on the actions. In the process, individuals maximize their success and happiness, and live the ultimate life.

So all the world's problems, including the most serious ones, can be solved by simply teaching everyone the skill of MPSSOT. Or in other words, all the world's problems can be solved by simply teaching everyone to be an ultimate person.

The Ultimate Life

Learning the skill of MPSSOT will benefit you personally in numerous ways. Collectively, these benefits define the ultimate life. Here are the primary ways that the skill of maximum problem solving skill over time will benefit you personally:

1) *Maximum success in all areas of your life* – You will become an expert at clearly identifying problems and solutions (action lists). You will learn how to take on tough problems by breaking them down into simple doable actions. And you will learn how to maximize performance on the doable actions. This includes problems in all areas of your life – both professional and personal.

2) *Maximum happiness* – The science of happiness shows us that action performance and emotional experience are directly linked. You will learn the conditions of maximum happiness and how to apply these conditions to your everyday life activities. There are three primary conditions of maximum happiness as specified in Flow Theory (see Appendix A2 for an overview of Flow Theory). These three conditions are:

> a) *clear goals* – this provides the necessary structure and direction to the activity
> b) *clear and immediate feedback* – this helps negotiate any challenging demands and allows adjustments to performance to maintain a Flow state
> c) *a balance between challenge and skill* – this balance provides a feeling a confidence and control over one's activities

3) *Maximum success and happiness over time* – The skill of MPSSOT has a built-in feedback mechanism that facilitates critical feedback on problem solving performance. This feedback is then used to correct mistakes, adapt to change, and improve both performance and happiness over time. The world is continuously

changing, so being adaptive to change is critical. The science of feedback systems is defined by Control Theory. An overview of Control Theory is given in Appendix A1.

4) *Future proofing yourself* - As you will learn in Chapter 3, the skill of MPSSOT is a necessary skill – for individuals, for businesses, and for the world. It will be therefore be mandatory learning for everyone in the future. By learning the skill of the future, you will be prepared for the future, and you can apply your knowledge of the future to your advantage in the present. You can avoid wasted time and energy on short term fads and focus on the things that matter. The future defines the things that will last over time and thereby defines the things that matter in human affairs.

5) *Prestige of being the best of all time* – An Ultimate Person is a best person of all time by definition. After completing the online course, you will become a true, certified Ultimate Person, backed by science. You will have the satisfaction of knowing that you are truly the best of all time.

6) *Help save the world* – The skill of maximum problem solving skill over time has a built-in guidance system for aligning your personal actions with the human survival problem and thereby helps you to save the world. Pandemics are an example of a human survival problem. Appendix B entitled Essential Workforce, provides an example of occupations that are aligned with the human survival problem. It lists the occupations that are essential for dealing with pandemics such as the Coronavirus pandemic.

7) *A certificate you can be proud of* – After completing the online course, you will obtain a certificate of your significant achievement. See the sample certificate in Appendix D. This will certify that you have completed the Ultimate Person courses, which is one of the most important and most valuable courses of all time.

It is an achievement that you can be proud of and will want to share with others.

2

HOW TO BE
AN ULTIMATE PERSON

This chapter defines how anyone can be an ultimate person. We know from Chapter 1 that that the scientific definition of the Ultimate Person is *a person who maximizes problem solving skill over time*, and we know the five key features of the skill of maximum problem solving skill over time. This chapter focuses on how to put this skill into practice on a daily basis.

The Ultimate Person Performance Process

The skill of MPSSOT is put into practice by means of the Ultimate Person Performance Process (UPPP). The UPPP is an iterative, step-by-step process for on-going action performance. Remember that solutions to problems are identified in terms of an action list. The UPPP is basically an action list management process that has six steps:

1) Define problems – this step involves defining the problems in detail. There are two categories of problems for an Ultimate Person – personal and professional. Personal problems are centered around establishing and maintaining self-sufficiency. Professional problems are centered around your occupation;

2) Define solutions (actions) – this step involves defining the solutions (i.e. actions) in detail. Be sure to use action words to define the action as well as measurements, deadlines and other details to define the actions (solution) in detail. The key is to define the actions in terms of being "doable" so that they can be successfully performed on the first try;

3) Perform solutions (actions) – this step involves performing the actions according to the Ultimate Person Performance Rules, which are detailed in the next section of this book;

4) Evaluate results – this step involves evaluating the results of your performance. Your action performance results provide valuable feedback on your progress so keep track of your results carefully. If you succeeded on the first try, congratulate yourself and move on to the next action. If you did not succeed on your first try, then you need to either repeat the action or redefine it so that it is more doable. Note that many actions, especially complex actions, will not be successfully performed on the first try, so please factor this into your expectations. Also note that there is plenty of options and support to help you succeed. A key characteristic of the Ultimate Person is the ability to turn negative feedback into positive results;

5) Repeat steps 2-4 continuously on new solutions. Note that the problems defined in Step 1 are pretty standard and will not change much - unless you undergo a life or career change. Steps 2-4 are where most of the on-going action takes place;

6) Perfect The UPPP and Have fun. Practice the UPPP on a daily basis and perfect it. Day by day, you will become better and better at it. It will not take long until you have mastered the skill of MPSSOT, which is one of the most valuable skills you will ever learn. It is the key to living the ultimate life!

The Ultimate Person Performance Rules

The UPPP uses performance rules designed to maximize performance in a way that also leads to maximum happiness. The performance rules are based primarily on Flow Theory which is a scientific theory of the psychology of optimal experience (i.e. maximum happiness). According to Flow Theory (see Appendix A2), action performance and happiness are directly linked. Here is an overview of this happiness/performance link.

The Happiness/Performance Link

By arranging actions according the guidelines of Flow theory, both performance and happiness will be maximized. A "Flow" state is characterized by three primary conditions:

1) *clear goals* – this provides the necessary structure and direction to the activity
2) *clear and immediate feedback* – this helps negotiate any challenging demands and allows adjustments to performance to maintain a Flow state
3) *a challenge/skill balance (CS balance)* – this provides a feeling of confidence and control over one's ability to succeed.

THE CHALLENGE/SKILL (CS) BALANCE

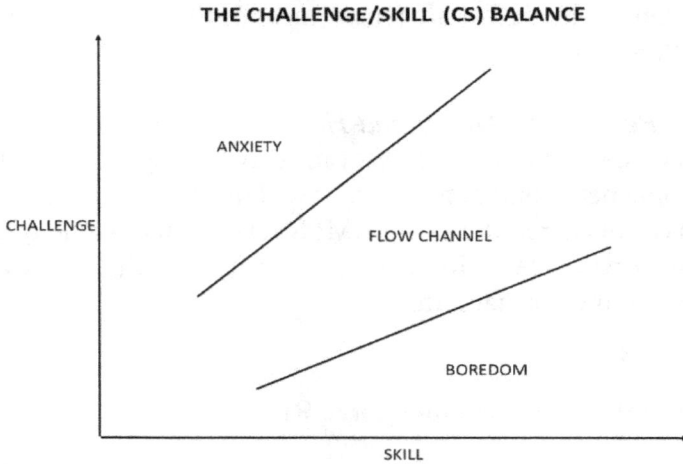

The challenge/skill balance diagram illustrates how the difference levels of challenge and skill affect one's mental state.

Above is a basic chart that summarizes the challenge/skill (CS) balance. It is a chart of the level of the challenge of a certain action versus the skill level available to meet the challenge. Notice that an activity that has high challenge and low skill leads to a state of anxiety or being stressed out because that action cannot be performed. Anxiety has a negative effect on performance because it can cause frustration with an activity that will eventually cause a person to give up and quit the activity.

An activity that has low challenge and high skill leads to a state of boredom because the activity is too easily performed. Boredom has a negative effect on performance because it can cause a person to lose interest and eventually quit the activity. In both states – anxiety and boredom – the key performance problem is lost attention and focus on the activity.

By contrast, the CS balance or "flow channel" has a positive effect on performance because a person is succeeding at an activity and increasing skill over time, so that higher levels of performance can be achieved over time. In a Flow state, attention and focus on the activity are maximized.

There are many other psychological benefits to optimal action performance including self-esteem, self-confidence, and an increased learning capacity. There is also evidence that these psychological benefits have medical benefits as well, although medical issues are beyond the scope of this book.

The Rules

There are four primary performance rules for all individuals. These performance rules are based on the three conditions of Flow mentioned above, plus safety awareness. Here is the list of Ultimate Person performance rules:

1) Clearly identify actions
2) Obtain feedback on progress
3) Maintain a challenge/skill balance
4) Maintain safety awareness

Performance Rule #1 Clearly identify actions.

Performance Rule #1 is necessary because clear goals are a condition of Flow. All actions should be based on a goal, which is basically the problem that needs to be solved. Actions (solutions) should be defined in terms of doable actions, and include a success measure and a time deadline for solving the problem.

Performance Rule #2 Obtain feedback on progress

Performance Rule #2 is necessary because feedback on progress is a condition of Flow. Even negative feedback is important because it helps you identify the areas where improvement may be necessary. Turning negative feedback into a positive learning experience is a key characteristic of the Ultimate Person. Remember that your primary source of feedback is your performance results on your daily actions.

Performance Rule #3 Maintain challenge/skill balance

Performance Rule #3 is necessary because a challenge/skill (CS) balance is a condition of Flow. It involves making adjustments to both the challenge and skill level to stay in a flow state, thereby avoiding the states of anxiety and boredom.

There are three basic guidelines for maintaining a CS balance:

1) *if you are in a state of anxiety, then either decrease challenge or increase skill or both*. The way to decrease challenge is to perform less actions in more time. Ways to increase skill are: a) try again (practice makes perfect); or b) break down actions into smaller, easier actions that are more doable. This can be accomplished by getting how-to information on the problem from an expert (either online or local); or c) getting UPPP skill training or re-training.

2) *if you are in a state of boredom, then increase challenge*. Ways to increase challenge include performing more actions in less time.

3) *always increase skill*. Increasing skill is always necessary to maintain a CS balance over time. This is because increasing skill is a strategy that will always move one closer to the CS balance *over time*, regardless of whether one is stressed out or bored. Life's challenges have a way of increasing themselves on their own.

Performance Rule #4 Maintain Safety Awareness

Performance Rule #4 is necessary because a Flow state can result in complete absorption of a person's attention. One must always maintain awareness of their surroundings to be able to respond to safety hazards. Texting while driving is a common example of a safety hazard that results from not maintaining awareness of one's surroundings. An effective way to maintain safety awareness is to always remember the slogan "safety first."

The Ultimate Person Action List

The ultimate person action list puts you in control of your life. It is a written document that helps you manage your actions over time. You can think of it as a control panel for all your life's activities. It provides control by means of the detailed problem solving information that can be continuously evaluated and adjusted as necessary to maximize success over time.

UP Action List Format

The UP Action List is structured in terms of lists and sections. There are two lists: one for UP personal actions; and one for UP professional actions. And there are two sections for each list: daily tasks and projects.

Your UP Personal Action List will have a section for daily personal tasks, and one for personal projects. Your UP Professional Action List will have a section for daily professional tasks, and one for professional projects. The daily task lists are a list of actions that are to be completed each day. These actions are typically simple, routine, but necessary tasks with a deadline of "end of the day." The project lists are lists of more complex actions that will take time to complete. Projects will typically have sub-tasks that will also take time (more than one day) to complete.

Personal vs. Professional Projects and Daily Tasks

Personal projects and daily tasks are pretty standard activities for everyone. What is new here is the need for continuous

MPSSOT skill development. So there are now four basic personal projects: 1) Continuous MPSSOT Skill Development; 2) Maintain Health; 3) Maintain Finances; and 4) Maintain Family.

Personal Project #1 Continuous MPSSOT Skill Development is the focus of this book. Personal Project #2 Maintain Health is beyond the scope of this book. Personal Project #3 Maintain Finances is beyond the scope of this book. Personal Project #4 Maintain Family is beyond the scope of this book, except to mention that sharing Ultimate Person education at www.ultimateperson.com is one of the best things you can do for a family member. All of these personal projects and even some of personal daily tasks have already been entered into the Ultimate Person Personal Action List forms for you (see next section on forms).

Professional projects and daily tasks are related to your occupation. If you are already employed, then you must follow the projects and daily tasks specified by your employer -- that is, if you want to keep your job. Ask your supervisor for a performance review. It provides valuable feedback on your job performance. If you are self-employed, then you must complete the professional projects and daily task forms yourself. Applying the principles of MPSSOT to your business will help you succeed and enjoy your business to a much greater extent.

The Ultimate Person Action List Forms

The next four pages consist of forms to use for your UP Personal Action List and your UP Professional Action List. Using your favorite word processor, Microsoft Word, or Google Docs, create a four page document, one page for each of the four forms. Print out a blank four page set. Then handwrite your tasks, projects, sub-tasks and deadline dates. Then type in your handwritten information. Congratulations, you have completed your first Ultimate Person Action List!

Notice that all of the four personal projects and many of the personal project sub-tasks, and even a personal daily task, has already been entered onto the personal forms for you. This should help give you a nice kick start to your Ultimate Person Action List.

Now, every morning for the rest of your life, update the UP Action List. Note that your daily tasks will change every day, but your projects will not change very frequently. Use the project lists to generate new ideas for your daily tasks. This way you will complete your projects in a systematic, time efficient manner. Day by day you will get better at this. Over time, you will master the skill of *maximum problem solving skill over time.* And you will be surprised and how fun and rewarding this is.

Ultimate Person Personal Action List
Daily Tasks

Action Name	Deadline
1. Update UP Action List	Today
2.	Today
3.	Today
4.	Today
5.	Today
6.	Today
7.	Today
8.	Today
9.	Today
10.	Today

UP Action List – page 1

Ultimate Person Personal Action List
Projects

Project Name   Deadline

1. Maintain MPSSOT Skill Development

Sub-Task 1. Take Ultimate Person Online Course
Sub-Task 2. Take Ultimate World Online Course
Sub-Task 3. Continuous MPSSOT Skill Development

2. Maintain Health
Sub-Task 1. Establish and maintain a healthy lifestyle
Sub-Task 2. Get expert health advice online or local
Sub-Task 3.

3. Maintain Finances
Sub-Task 1. Establish and maintain an essential job or business
Sub-Task 2. Get expert financial advice online or local
Sub-Task 3.

4. Maintain Family
Sub-Task 1. Share UP Education at www.ultimateperson.com
Sub-Task 2. Get expert family advice online or local
Sub-Task 3.

UP Action List – page 2

Ultimate Person Professional Action List
Daily Tasks

Action Name	Deadline
1.	Today
2.	Today
3.	Today
4.	Today
5.	Today
6.	Today
7.	Today
8.	Today
9.	Today
10.	Today

Ultimate Person Professional Action List
Projects

Project Name   Deadline

1.

      Sub-Task 1.
      Sub-Task 2.
      Sub-Task 3.

2.

      Sub-Task 1.
      Sub-Task 2.
      Sub-Task 3.

3.

      Sub-Task 1.
      Sub-Task 2.
      Sub-Task 3.

4.

      Sub-Task 1.
      Sub-Task 2.
      Sub-Task 3.

Practical Tips For Managing The UP Action List

This section on practical tips provides tips on the following four topics: getting focused; getting things done; getting relevant; and computer support.

Getting Focused

It is now known that focused attention is the key to both success and happiness. This section focuses on how to use the UP action list to maintain focused attention over time. When using your UP action list, keep the following three things in mind: a) make consistent progress; b) stay positive over time; and c) add in down time.

Making Consistent Progress

Try to accomplish at least one UP action each day, even if it is only a very small thing. Big things are not accomplished in a day. Big things are accomplished by doing small things each day. Document your small accomplishments by making notes on your UP Action List document. Then update and print out a clean copy of UP Action List regularly (e.g. weekly). These regular, consistent updates to your UP Action List are an essential part of your new ultimate lifestyle. They will become a nice, positive start to each day, every day for life.

Can you imagine what would happen if everyone in the world did at least one UP action each day? The Ultimate World would be realized and all the world's problems would be solved.

Staying Positive Over Time

Action performance failures provide critical feedback and indicates areas where attention is needed. The most successful leaders all share one common trait -- they know how to turn negative feedback (failures on specific actions) into positive results.

Successful people know that expecting continuous positive feedback is setting yourself up for failure and anxiety. Factor this into your expectations and stay positive <u>over time</u>.

This is where the UP Performance Rules and Practical Tips fit in. Use the UP Performance Rules and Practical Tips to turn the negative feedback into positive results and get through the performance obstacles.

Add In Down Time

It is impossible to stay 100% focused, 100% of the time. Schedule down time from your UP Action List and get some rest and relaxation. Many people find that they can focus better in the morning when the mind is clear and refreshed, so morning time is typically the best time to work on your UP action list. Then try to accomplish at least one UP action during the remainder of the day and make a handwritten note on your UP Action List document. Later in the day is typically a good time for rest and relaxation and getting prepared for the next day. Practicing your UP Action List will help you pinpoint your high performance times of the day, so that you will then know the best time to perform tasks and the best time to relax.

Getting Things Done

Getting Things Done is a time management methodology based on the concept of moving planned tasks and projects out of the mind by recording them externally, and then breaking them down into actionable work items. This allows attention to be focused on taking action on tasks, instead of recalling them.

It was first published in the book "Getting Things Done" by David Allen in 2001, and then revised in 2015 to reflect the applicable research in cognitive science. The latest edition is highly recommended reading. You will get more time management techniques than you can use.

Allen recommends setting up a dedicated workstation for organizing paperwork. This includes folders for each project and a paper tray to supply the paperwork for the next task to be completed. Because computer technology is rapidly changing, it is essential to have a paperwork system as a baseline.

It is becoming increasingly clear in the cognitive science that the mind works best when it is able to concentrate fully on one task, thereby eliminating all distractions. This is the opposite of multi-tasking. Once the necessary tasks are completed, then multi-tasking is helpful for information gathering.

Getting Relevant

To the Ultimate Person, relevance means relevance to the human survival problem. The human survival problem provides guidance and direction to the things that everyone needs to be working on. Remember that one of the five features of the skill of MPSSOT is direct relevance to the human survival problem.

Relevance is addressed in the Ultimate Person Action List in the "professional problem solving skill" section. Basically, relevance is defined in terms of your job or occupation.

What are the jobs that are relevant to the human survival problem? These jobs are determined by the Essential Workforce. Please see Appendix B for an excellent example of an Essential Workforce. This list of jobs or occupations was published by the State of California in March of 2020 as the essential jobs that were to remain in force during the early stages of the Coronavirus pandemic. All other jobs or occupations were deemed non-essential and were to be shut down by law.

Pandemics are a human survival problem and the Coronavirus (COVID-19) pandemic provides an excellent example of how a human survival problem takes priority in world events.

Although many non-essential jobs have since reopened, everyone should plan on moving into an Essential Workforce job. This does not mean that you should immediately quit a non-essential job. After all, you have short term bills to pay (housing, food, transportation, etc.). It means that everyone should be getting prepared to move into an essential job or business. This is because eventually, all non-essential jobs and businesses will be phased out. It's a matter of human survival.

Computer Support

There is plenty of computer support available for your UP Action List with a lot more to come. This support falls into three primary areas: 1) managing the UP Action List document; 2) how-to information; and 3) ultimate computer support.

Managing Your UP Action List Document

It is important to have a hard copy of your UP Action List document. Having this hard copy frees your mind from the burden of constantly remembering it. Then you can use your mind for getting a few important things done each day.

All you really need is a word processor for typing the initial action list and editing it on a daily basis. Although there are specialized apps for managing to-do lists available, they require extra effort to manage the list and this extra effort may not provide much more benefit than a basic word processor. Also, most of the to-do list apps do not fit the UP Action List format. Finally, and most importantly, your UP Action List Document allows you to focus strictly on being an Ultimate Person, without all the other distractions on your cell phone.

How-To Information

There is plenty of useful how-to information on the internet – you just need to know where to find it. How-to websites give specific actions (solutions) for solving specific problems. Examples include wikihow.com and howtodothings.com. Even basic Google search and YouTube now include a lot of how-to information.   Solutions (action lists) to most everyday problems are already available. Use these proven solutions as the source for many of your UP projects and daily actions. There is no need to reinvent the wheel on your UP activities.

Ultimate Computer Support

The ultimate computer support will come from the Human Survival Problem Solver (HSPS). The HSPS is an intelligent computer system to identify and solve human survival problems and sub-problems. It is also known as the future of internet.

The HSPS, when implemented, will automate all of your daily problem solving activity in an intelligent fashion. Basically, you will just enter certain problems into the system, and it will supply you with intelligent solutions to the problems, along with support information (readings, videos, etc.) on how to best perform the solutions. All activity in the HSPS is directly linked to the human survival problem.

For more information on the HSPS, see the following two sections in this book: Appendix A3 *Ultimate World Theory*; and Chapter 3 *The Future of the Internet*.

Benefit Summary of The Ultimate Person Action List

As if the list of benefits of being an Ultimate Person (and living the Ultimate Life) are not enough, here are some more benefits that are specific to the UP action list.

1) *Less stress* – Lists can directly reduce your stress level. Fewer surprises. Fewer tight deadlines. Less rushing from task-to-task and place-to-place.

2) *Get more done* – When you are aware of the right things to do, you are better able to get things done. You get more of the right things done in less time.

3) *Fewer mistakes* – Forgotten items, details, and instructions lead to extra work.

4) *Fewer problems* – Being disorganized actually creates new problems for yourself. Avoid creating your own problems.

5) *More free time* – Getting the right things done on time means more free time for yourself.

6) *Less wasted time* – When you know what you need to do, you waste less time on things that don't matter. Instead of wondering what you should do next, you are already steps ahead on the things to do matter.

7) *More opportunities* – Being on top of your time and work produces more opportunities. The early bird always has more options and luck favors the prepared.

8) *Improve your reputation* – At work and life you become known as reliable.

9) *Less work* – A common misconception is that to-do lists are just extra work. To the contrary, to-do lists make your life easier. Everything takes less effort when you know what to do in advance.

10) *More time on the things that matter* – To-do lists allow you to spend your time on the things that matter.

11) *Help save the world* – You actually help save the world by working on UP actions and following the UP Performance Rules because they have built-in relevance to the human survival problem.

3

WHY EVERYONE NEEDS TO BE AN ULTIMATE PERSON

As if the outstanding benefits of being an Ultimate Person is not enough incentive, here is another incentive . . . it's mandatory. The reasoning for why it is mandatory, and not just desirable, for everyone in the world to become an Ultimate Person is as simple as 1-2-3.

First, Ultimate Person education provides the knowledge individual people need in order to maximize their individual problem solving skill over time.

Second, all individual people need to maximize their problem solving skill over time in order for the world as a whole to maximize its group problem solving skill over time.

Third, the world as a whole needs to maximize its group problem solving skill over time to resolve the maximum complexity of the human survival problem.

The bottom line is that the complexity of the human survival problem requires maximum problem solving skill from the human species as a whole, and subsequently from all individual people. It is therefore mandatory for everyone to become an Ultimate Person. It is *do or die* for the human species!

Scientifically speaking, this mandatory nature of Ultimate Person education is the central hypothesis of Ultimate World Theory. See Appendix A3, page 61, for this exact hypothesis, and for an overview of Ultimate World Theory.

The Human Survival Problem

So, what exactly is the human survival problem? The human survival problem is the most complex problem imaginable to humans. It is characterized in terms of two types of threats to human survival – natural and artificial. Let us start with the natural threats. The most obvious natural threat comes from the sun which is heating up over time and will eventually burn out, making life on earth uninhabitable along the way. We can reasonably certain about this because the sun is a star similar to numerous other stars in the universe, and behaves similar to these other stars which heat up and burn out over time. By observing other stars at different points in their life cycle, we can predict the life cycle of the sun with a reasonable amount of accuracy.

See the following chart showing the life cycle of the sun, from its formation as a baby star to its death as a white dwarf, approximately 13 billion years later. We can see that, unfortunately, life on earth has a limited time. This chart points out the approximate time for the end of life on earth. The good news is that this endpoint is about 2.5 billion years from now, which gives us plenty of time to implement the solution.

Life Cycle of the Sun

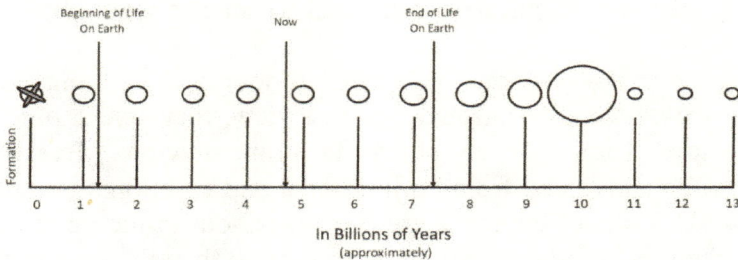

In Billions of Years
(approximately)

Other less severe natural threats include space objects such as meteors and asteroids, which can harm the earth and its atmosphere upon impact. And there is also the threat of a pandemic of infectious disease that can quickly spread across the world. The Coronavirus pandemic illustrates the devastating impact of a pandemic. A more severe virus could cause human extinction, thereby making pandemics an urgent survival problem.

Now for the artificial threats. The most obvious artificial threat is the social problem of human conflicts around the world, which manifests itself in terms of war and violence. These conflicts could escalate and lead to extinction of the human species. Most scientists agree that the threat of nuclear war is the single greatest threat to humans.

Implications of Human Extinction

Human extinction would be the most catastrophic event imaginable to humans. It would be the complete end of the human species. There are four primary implications:

1) an inconceivably large number of human lives would
be lost by not being born;
2) the significance of the lives of all the billions of people
alive today would be lost:
3) the significance of the lives of all the billions of our
ancestors would be lost;
4) everything in history associated with being human, including all culture, all art, and all science would be lost.

If one is not convinced of the importance of human survival from a strictly rational point of view, then one should be
convinced from a strictly emotional point of view. Everyone
should be convinced from both rational and emotional points of
view. Despite all the problems we hear about in the news each
day, there is no other problem more serious than the human survival problem.

The Human Survival Solution

So the human survival problem is the most serious and
most complex problem imaginable to humans. This is the bad
news.

Now for the good news. The good news is that there is a
solution to the human survival problem, and the great news is that
the solution is very simple. It is the same solution as the one that
solves all the other problems in the world. The solution is simply
to have everyone learn the skill of maximum problem solving
skill over time by reading this book, taking the online Ultimate
Person Course at www.ultimateperson.com and then sharing the
course with others. For an explanation of how this solution will
work, please review the section entitled *The Simple Solution to
All the World's Problems*, on page 8 of this book.

Key Predictions For The Future

The knowledge that Ultimate Person education is mandatory education for everyone is extremely powerful knowledge. It can be used to accurately predict the future.

As mentioned above, the bottom line on why Ultimate Person education is mandatory education for everyone is because it is a matter of human survival. The fact that Ultimate Person education is a matter of human survival means that it can be accurately predicted to occur in the future. This is because human survival issues are safety issues (i.e. the ultimate safety issues), and safety issues always take priority over all other issues in human affairs. The Coronavirus pandemic shows precisely how a human survival problem takes priority in world events.

There are currently 70 scientific predictions for the future, each derived from a distinct hypothesis, detailed in the book entitled *The Ultimate World*. Here are five of the primary predictions:

> The Person of the Future – the person of the future, in terms of the skill set required for the future, is the Ultimate Person. The official definition of an Ultimate Person is a person who maximizes problem solving skill over time. This book is the definitive book on the Ultimate Person.

> The World of the Future – the world of the future, in terms of how people will socialize and interact, is The Ultimate World. The official definition of the Ultimate World is a world-wide group of Ultimate People who work together as a team to maximize group problem solving skill over time. The definitive book on the ultimate world is *The Ultimate World*, which is the textbook for the online course on the Ultimate World, available at www.ultimateperson.com.

The Future Economy – the economy of the future, in terms of the businesses and jobs of the future, is The Space Life Economy. The Space Life Economy is defined as a space based economy similar to the current earth based economy. It is helpful to think of today's economy as a space based economy that is in earth mode.

The Future of Communication – the future of communication, in terms of the format of communication, is Ultimate World Experiments. Ultimate World Experiments are defined as a scientific experiment that tests the necessity of an action. Ultimate World Experiments are the means by which actions are clearly identified and validated, and clearly identifying and validating actions will be the focus of all formal communication in the future. In essence, all formal communication in the future will focus on identifying the "do or die" actions for the world. Again, it's a matter of human survival. Without Ultimate World Experiments, the world will not know the actions are "do or die" for the world, and therefore will not know to perform them. If the "do or die" actions are not performed, then the human species will go extinct, and there will be no future.

A simplified version of communication in the future is people saying one of two things to each other: 1) we need to do this because it is necessary for human survival; or 2) we don't need to do this because it is not necessary for human survival. Ultimate World Experiments will be the means in which people communicate in a civilized, constructive, and credible fashion, as opposed to today's opinionated bickering.

The Future of Technology – The technology of the future, in terms of the information technology such as the internet and individual computing devices such as personal computers and cell phones, is the Human Survival Problem Solver. The Human Survival Problem Solver is defined as a world-wide computer based solutions manager for managing all human survival problems in all safe locations of the universe and all time. It is also known as the future of the internet. The underlying science of the HSPS has already been defined and published in *The Ultimate World*, and the HSPS was patented by Carmen Tripodi in 2020. The next section explains why the HSPS is the future of the internet.

The Future of the Internet

The internet originated in the 1960s as a computer network research project by the United States Department of Defense. Its original name was ARPANET (Advanced Research Projects Agency Network). The original users were from the United States military and academia in the 1970s. It gradually expanded to commercial users from around the world. The early 1990s marked the beginning of the modern internet and its use has since expanded exponentially into virtually every aspect of modern life.

The future of the internet is the Human Survival Problem Solver (HSPS). The reason the HSPS is the future of the internet is because it is a matter of human survival. Human survival problems are the ultimate safety problems and safety problems always take priority in world events. The Coronavirus pandemic is an excellent example of how a human survival problem takes priority in world events.

Human survival problems are complex problems and require intelligent reasoning on the actions necessary to solve them. The HSPS provides the necessary intelligent reasoning in a computer system, in the safest most effective fashion. As an intelligent problem solving computer system that focuses directly on human survival problems, the HSPS must take priority in all computer systems, including the internet. The bottom line is that the HSPS has to be the future of the internet. Again, it is a matter of human survival.

The HSPS will benefit the world in numerous ways. Three of the primary ways are by: uniting the world; social responsibility, and safety.

Uniting The World

The HSPS will unite the world in two primary ways:

1. A clear focus on a common goal of all humans – Human survival is a common goal of everyone around the world regardless of nationality, race, sex, religion, or any other demographic category. The HSPS ensures that all activity in the system is focused directly on this common goal.

2. By facilitating individual contributions to the common goal by identifying specific sub-problems of human survival problems and the specific actions necessary to solve them. The HSPS empowers everyone in the world to use their special expertise to help solve the human survival problem.

Social Responsibility

The HSPS enhances social responsibility by solving the world's social problems. Many of the world's social problems are conflict related (e.g. racism, sexism, poverty) and the HSPS solves these social problems by eliminating the conflict. Conflict is eliminated via the focus on the common goal of human survival, and by facilitating teamwork toward achieving the common goal. The HSPS is operationalized as a world-wide problem solving team, similar to a sports team. All the conflict related problems are automatically solved because conflict between individual team members is eliminated.

Safety

The HSPS enhances safety in three primary ways:

1. By solving the ultimate safety problems – Human survival problems are the ultimate safety problems and the HSPS is an intelligent computer system specially designed to solve human survival problems. The HSPS is the ultimate safety system.

2. By focusing strictly on human survival problems – this eliminates problems with erratic, unsafe, and irrelevant data.

3. By prioritizing human programming over machine programming. Machine Learning is currently a very popular computer programming technique in the field of Artificial Intelligence (AI). However, the use of Machine Learning (i.e. machine programming) on human survival problems is a major safety problem because it would allow the computer to make human survival decisions on its own. In the HSPS, machine programming is secondary to human programming.

The Benefits of Knowing the Future

Knowing the future has tremendous benefits. Here are some of the primary ones:

1) knowing the future helps you make good decisions in the present. You know where to spend your time, energy and money;

2) knowing the future helps you avoid wasted time, energy and money;

3) knowing the future helps you avoid the stress of jumping from short term fad to short term fad;

4) knowing the future provides a clear sense of direction in your life;

5) knowing the future provides the satisfaction of knowing your life matters. The things that matter in life are the things that stand the test of time. The future defines the things that will stand the test of time and therefore defines the things that matter;

6) knowing the future provides the satisfaction of knowing that you can be a true ultimate person and truly live the ultimate life, and obtain all its tremendous benefits. Please refer to the sections on *The Ultimate Life* (page 10) and *The Ultimate Person Action List* (page 31) for a reminder of these tremendous benefits.

CONCLUSION

This book defines the what, how, why and when of the Ultimate Person. Here is a quick summary of each.

The What - The Ultimate Person is defined in terms of the best behavior of all time. The best behavior of all time is problem solving behavior because it leads directly to solutions to human problems. This includes the most serious problems in the world such as war, violence, poverty, racism and sexism. Above all, it includes the solution to the most serious problem facing humans – the human survival problem. The scientific definition of the ultimate person is *a person who maximizes problem solving skill over time*. This definition is detailed in chapter 1.

The How – The skill of *maximum problem solving skill over time* is put into practice by means of the Ultimate Person Performance Process (UPPP). The UPPP is an iterative action performance process for on-going action performance. The UPPP is managed on a daily basis by means of the Ultimate Person Action list. The process of managing the Ultimate Person Action list on a daily basis is detailed in chapter 2.

The Why – The primary reason for why everyone in the world must become an Ultimate Person is because it is a matter of human survival. The human survival problem is the ultimate problem. The human survival problem and solution are detailed in chapter 3.

This mandatory nature of Ultimate Person education has major implications for the world. All organizations, including all businesses, all universities, and the entire world as a whole, must master the skill of *maximum problem solving skill over time*. Again it is a matter of human survival, or in other words, it is do or die for the world.

The fact that the skill of *maximum problem solving skill over time* is a matter of human survival means that it can be accurately predicted to occur in the future. This is because human survival is a safety issue (it's the ultimate safety issue) and safety issues always take priority in human affairs. The Coronavirus pandemic shows precisely how a human survival problem takes priority in world events.

The Time To Be An Ultimate Person is Now

The When – The time for everyone to become an ultimate person is now. Now is the correct time for three primary reasons:

> 1) the what, how and why have now been scientifically defined;

> 2) an online course to teach people how to become an ultimate person is now available free of charge to the world;

> 3) the sooner the better – the sooner people begin to master the skill of *maximum problem solving skill over time*, the sooner the world's problems will get solved. The

sooner people begin, the less human pain and suffering, and less human conflict there will be.

4) And finally, the sooner people begin to master the skill of *maximum problem solving skill over time,* the sooner people will obtain all the tremendous benefits of being an Ultimate Person.

Specifically, here are two things you need to do now: 1) register and pass the Ultimate Person online course at www.ultimateperson.com; and 2) share your achievement with everyone you know. Sharing is simple, just refer everyone you know to www.ultimateperson.com. Remember that sharing *The Ultimate Person* book and online course means a lot more than just sharing your outstanding achievement with your friends. It will actually help solve the world's problems because you will be sharing the solution to all the world's problems.

Sharing the Ultimate Person education is one of the best, easiest, and least expensive (it's free!) ways to help other people. This is great news for people who like to help others. Isn't this you?

APPENDECES

Appendix A. Core Science References

A1. Control Theory
A2. Flow Theory
A3. Ultimate World Theory

Appendix B. Essential Workforce

Appendix C. Sample Certificates

Appendix D. Glossary

CONTROL THEORY

Control theory is a general theory of feedback systems. The overall theme of control theory is the use of feedback to maintain stability in a system over time. It originated in engineering and mathematics, and evolved into use by the social sciences, such as economics, psychology, and sociology. The theoretical basis for control theory was first described by James Clerk Maxwell in 1868 and has since gone through a number of refinements.

A system is a generic entity for something that takes inputs, processes the inputs in some fashion, and then produces a desired result called an output. The word "system" is a generic term that could apply to anything that processes inputs. For example, a food processor is a system for processing ingredients from a recipe (the input) into finished food ready for consumption (the output). A common application of a food processor is fresh salsa. The ingredients of fresh salsa include tomatoes, onions, garlic, chili peppers, and cilantro. The food processor (the

system) chops and blends the ingredients (the inputs) which produces the desired result of fresh salsa (the output).

A SYSTEM

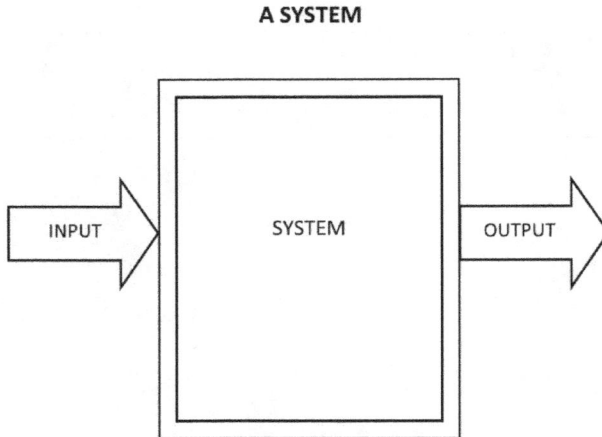

This system diagram illustrates the three elements of a generic system:
the input, the output, and the system.

A control system takes the output of a system, uses this
output as feedback and makes corrections to the output based a
desired goal, called a reference. The control element is called the
controller. Notice in the control system diagram that the output
is fed back into the controller which compares the actual output
to the reference (the desired output), and makes corrections to the
output signal which is then input back to the system in a continuous cycle. Stability over time is achieved by using the feedback
to make corrections to any variance between the actual output
and the desired output. Over time, the variance between the actual output and the desired output is reduced until the desired output is achieved.

A CONTROL SYSTEM

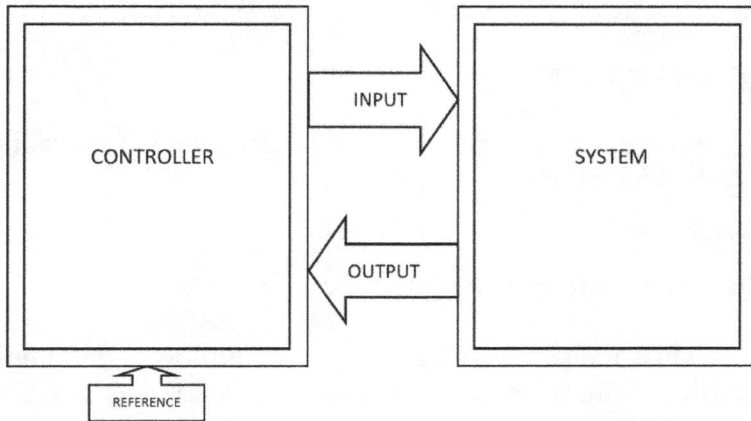

This control system diagram illustrates the framework of the five ele-
ments of a control system: the reference, the controller, the input, the
output, and the system.

Here are three typical examples of the application of control theory: a temperature control system, a speed control system,
and a health control system.

A Temperature Control System

All modern buildings have temperature control systems,
implemented in the form of a thermostat. The thermostat allows
the user to set a desired temperature and it automatically controls
the actual temperature of the building to match the desired temperature set by the user. The five control system elements of a
temperature control system are:

1) the reference – the desired temperature set by the user
2) the controller – the electronic control device of the
heating, ventilation, air conditioning (HVAC) unit

3) the input – the on/off signal to the heater or air conditioner within the HVAC unit
4) the output – the actual temperature of the air in the room
5) the system – the HVAC unit.

Stability over time is achieved by establishing and maintaining the desired temperature set by the user.

A Speed Control System

Most modern cars have speed control systems, implemented in the form of cruise control. A cruise control system allows the driver to set a desired speed and it automatically controls the actual speed of the car to match the desired speed. The five control system elements of a cruise control system are:

1) the reference – the desired speed set by the driver
2) the controller – the electronic control device of the fuel injector
3) the input – the fuel
4) the output – the actual speed of the car
5) the system – the engine.

Stability over time is achieved by establishing and maintaining the desired speed set by the driver.

A Health Control System

A common first line diagnostic test done by doctors when patients visit with symptoms of an illness, is the comprehensive metabolic panel (CMP). This lab test gives the doctor critical feedback on the patient's health based on a long list of heath variables such as glucose (blood sugar), and various nutrients (e.g. sodium). The doctor then controls the patient's health condition by prescribing medicine to bring the patient's health variables within the desired ranges. The five control system elements of this health control system are:

1) the reference – the desired ranges of the comprehensive metabolic panel (CMP)
2) the controller – the doctor
3) the input – the patient's blood sample
4) the output – the patient's laboratory report
5) the system – the laboratory.

Stability over time is achieved by establishing and maintaining the desired ranges of the CMP.

Relevance to The Ultimate Person

Control theory is relevant to the Ultimate Person by providing a useful feedback mechanism for managing the Ultimate Person Action List. By managing your UP Action List as a control system, similar to the settings on your computer, or the dashboard on your car, you can maximize your action performance over time.

It is especially useful for identifying information on performance problem areas (action performance failures or "negative feedback") and then using this information to make changes in either action identification or action performance, to turn these performance failures into performance successes. It thereby helps to ensure that problem solving skill <u>over time</u> is maximized.

Control theory also provides the framework for information management in Ultimate World Theory (see Appendix A3).

FLOW THEORY

Flow theory describes a mental state during performance of an action in which a person performing the action is fully immersed in a feeling of energized focus, full involvement and enjoyment in the process of the activity. The definitive book on Flow Theory is entitled *Flow: The Psychology of Optimal Experience*. Optimal experience is commonly known as the emotion called maximum happiness – the most positive of all emotions.

Mihaly Csikszentmihalyi is the author of Flow theory. He first published the concept of Flow in psychology in 1975, and then authored the definitive book mentioned above in 1990. He did extensive interviews and monitoring of people performing different types of activities in the search for the conditions of optimal experience. He found that there were three primary conditions of optimal experience:

1) *clear goals* – this provides the necessary structure and direction to the activity
2) *clear and immediate feedback* – this helps the person negotiate any challenging demands and allows them to make adjustments to their performance to maintain a flow state
3) *a balance between challenge and skill* – this balance provides a feeling of confidence and control over one's ability to succeed.

THE CHALLENGE/SKILL (CS) BALANCE

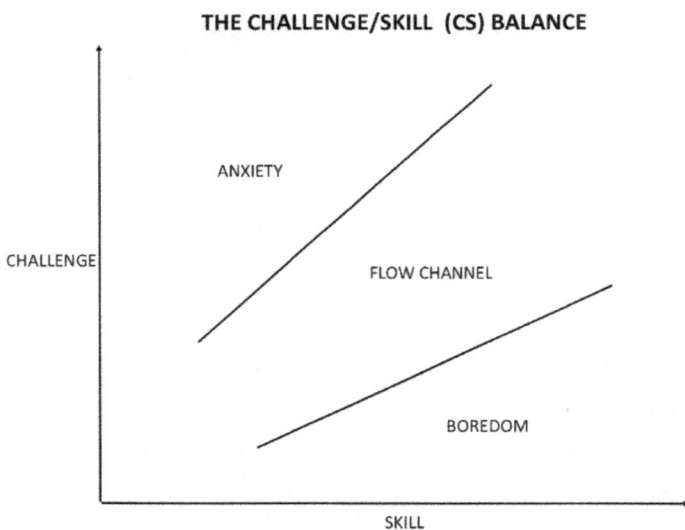

This challenge/skill balance diagram illustrates how the different levels of challenge and skill affect one's mental state.

The challenge/skill balance, or CS Balance, is the golden rule of Flow. The above chart illustrates the CS balance. It is a chart of the challenge level of a certain action versus the skill level available to meet the challenge. Notice that an activity that has high challenge and low skill leads to a state of anxiety or being stressed out because the action cannot be performed. Anxiety has a negative effect on performance because it can cause frustration with an activity that will eventually cause a person to give up and quit the activity.

An activity with low challenge and high skill leads to a state of boredom because the activity is too easily performed. Boredom has a negative effect on performance because it can cause a person to lose interest and eventually quit the activity. In both states – anxiety and boredom – the key performance problem is lost attention and focus on the activity.

By contrast, the CS balance or "flow channel" has a positive effect on performance because a person is succeeding at an activity and increasing skill over time, so that higher levels of performance can be achieved over time. In a Flow state, attention and focus on the activity are maximized.

Examples of Flow

By applying Flow theory to virtually any activity, both performance and happiness can be improved. Here are three examples of applying Flow theory: in sports, in music, and at work.

Flow In Sports

Sports offers plenty of opportunity to experience Flow. Here is how the three primary conditions of Flow apply to sports:

1) clear goals – win the game
2) clear and immediate feedback – the score of the game
3) CS Balance – improving the score by applying athletic skill. This also leads to increased enjoyment of the sport.

Athletes are known to use the following expressions to describe the Flow state: "in the zone," "unbeatable," and "on auto."

Flow In Music

Music also offers plenty of opportunity to experience Flow. Here is how the three primary conditions of Flow apply to music:

1) clear goals – the song's melody (structure) of musical notes
2) clear and immediate feedback – the actual sound of the musical instruments
3) CS Balance – improving the sound by applying musical skill. This also leads to increased enjoyment of the music.

Musicians are known to use the following expressions to describe the Flow state: "perfect harmony," "tuned in," and "jamming."

Flow At Work

Work also offers plenty of opportunity to experience Flow. Here is how the three primary conditions of Flow apply to work:

1) clear goals – performance targets such as sales and customer service ratings
2) clear and immediate feedback – actual performance results on the targets
3) CS Balance – improved performance on the targets by applying the skills of the workers. This also leads to increased enjoyment at work.

Businesses use the following expressions to describe the Flow state: "hit the mark," "better than expected earnings," and "crushing it."

Group Flow

Flow theory also applies to groups. Here is how the three primary conditions of Flow, apply to groups:

> 1) clear goals – the group goal
> 2) clear and immediate feedback – the group's performance results
> 3) CS Balance – improving the performance of the group by applying the skills of the group members. This also leads to increased enjoyment of the group experience.

Sports teams, music bands, business organizations, and virtually any group can benefit significantly from applying Flow Theory.

Relevance to The Ultimate Person

Flow Theory is relevant to The Ultimate Person by means of the Ultimate Person Performance Process (UPPP), and is directly integrated into the performance rules. The performance rules are justified by their necessity to facilitate a Flow experience.

Flow theory clearly demonstrates the link between action performance and emotional experience. The UPPP puts Flow Theory into practice, thereby helping to ensure that both performance and happiness are maximized.

ULTIMATE WORLD THEORY

Ultimate World Theory is a scientific theory of the ultimate world or the "best world of all time." The Ultimate World is scientifically defined as "a world-wide group of ultimate people who work together as a team to maximize group problem solving skill over time."

Ultimate World Theory was carefully defined using established scientific method which is the hallmark of credible science. Carmen Tripodi is the author of Ultimate World Theory, and the theory is published in the book entitled *The Ultimate World (2021)*.

The initial version of Ultimate World Theory consists of a set of 70 hypotheses all of which are derived from a primary hypothesis called The Supreme Hypothesis. The Supreme Hypothesis of Ultimate World Theory is stated as follows:

> *Establishing and maintaining UP$_{MAX}$ is a necessary action because of the maximum problem complexity of the human survival problem, which requires maximum group problem solving skill over time to resolve this maximum problem complexity.*

UP$_{MAX}$ is defined as the "maximum number of ultimate people" and an ultimate person is defined as "a person who maximizes problem solving skill over time." We can be certain that the complexity of the human survival problem is going to require maximum problem solving skill over time to solve it. This certainty on the need for maximum problem solving skill over time validates The Supreme Hypothesis of Ultimate World Theory. As Albert Einstein said when explaining his theory of relativity, "The theory is correct" (because the math is correct). As Carmen Tripodi says, "The theory is correct because the reasoning is sound and because it cannot be credibly denied. Anyone who claims that we are not going to need to maximize problem solving skill over time to survive this universe, is going to have credibility problems."

In simple terms, Ultimate World Theory can be explained using the following simple formula:

$$UW = UP_{MAX}$$

where UW stands for the Ultimate World and UP$_{MAX}$ stands for the maximum number of ultimate people.

Ultimate World Theory Diagram

The Ultimate World Theory diagram represents an informational roadmap of all the key elements of the theory, including the inputs, the outputs and the feedback loops. It is based on control theory framework which is an established theory of feed-back systems. The diagram shows how the people interact with the technology. The people interact with each other through the technology in the same way that people today interact with each other through the internet. The future of technology is the Human Survival Problem Solver and the future of people is the Ultimate World. Interestingly, the Ultimate World Theory diagram illustrates the solution to all the world's problems, all on one page.

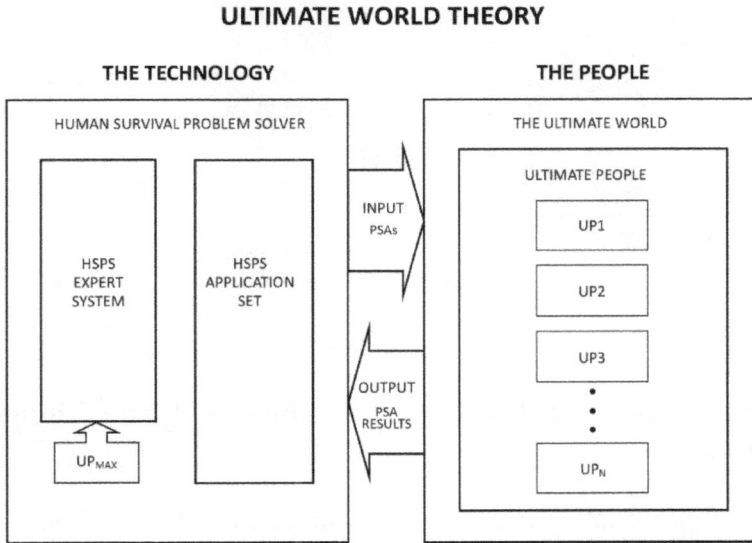

ULTIMATE WORLD THEORY

THE TECHNOLOGY	THE PEOPLE

HUMAN SURVIVAL PROBLEM SOLVER

THE ULTIMATE WORLD

ULTIMATE PEOPLE

HSPS EXPERT SYSTEM

HSPS APPLICATION SET

INPUT PSAs

UP1

UP2

UP3

OUTPUT PSA RESULTS

UP_{MAX}

UP_N

Ultimate Person Theory Diagram

The Ultimate Person Theory diagram zooms in on one of the UP units from the Ultimate World Theory diagram. This diagram is also based on the control theory framework. It shows the inputs – the problem solving actions (PSAs), and the outputs – the performance results. It also shows the system that transforms the inputs into the outputs – the Ultimate Person Performance Process. The Ultimate Person Performance Process is where the skill of maximum problem solving skill over time is put into practice.

ULTIMATE PERSON THEORY

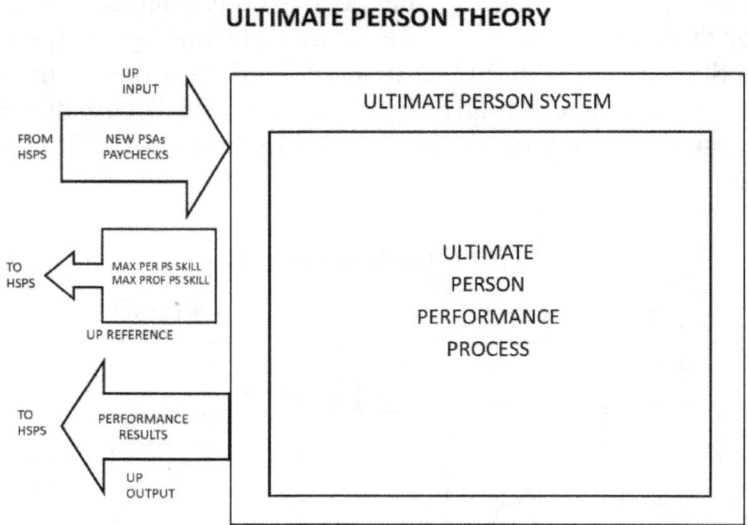

Relation Between The Ultimate People and The Ultimate World

The relation between The Ultimate People and The Ultimate World is *a system within a system.* The UPs and the UW utilize feedback by means of control theory, so the underlying theory for each system is control theory. Consequently, the relation between UPs and the UW is *a control system within a control system*, with the UPs being control systems within the UW control system. Control theory needs to be the underlying theory because control theory provides the means to exchange feedback between the UPs and UW for correcting mistakes, adapting to change, dealing with unknowns, maintaining stability, and improving performance over time.

To understand how control systems work, it is recommended to read Appendix A1. Note that the word "control" and "controller" in UW Theory are actually about maintaining "stability over time" in the Ultimate World. They are not about controlling people in an oppressive sense.

This relation of *a control system within a control system* facilitates systematic problem solving information flow between the Ultimate People and the Ultimate World, with the goal of maximizing individual and group problem solving skill over time, and the goal of maximizing individual and group happiness.

The New School of Science

One of the primary scientific innovations in Ultimate World Theory is the establishment of a new knowledge type called "necessitive knowledge."

The vast majority of science is descriptive and describes "the way things are." Necessitive science is different and defines "the way things need to be." The word "necessitive" is a new term that makes for a convenient comparison to the conventional descriptive science.

The validity of a descriptive theory is addressed by means of empirical studies or mathematical analysis. The validity of a necessitive theory is addressed by verifying the necessity of an action to solve a problem. In the UW Theory, the overall goal is solve the human survival problem, so validity is addressed by verifying the necessity of an action to solve the human survival problem (or sub-problem). In short, validity in necessitive science involves the simple statement – is it really do or die for the world?

So the new school of necessitive science is the science of do or die for the world. The Ultimate World scientific method, which is detailed in the book entitled *The Ultimate World*, puts this new science into practice. Note that necessitive science is not a replacement for descriptive science. It integrates descriptive science into it and focuses everything on solutions to human survival problems and sub-problems.

Ultimate World Theory vs. The Theory of Everything

The Theory of Everything is a descriptive theory of physics that fully explains and integrates all physical aspects of the universe. Current efforts to find the Theory of Everything are focused on integrating the physics of the very big (General Relativity) and the very small (Quantum Mechanics). However, since General Relativity and Quantum Mechanics are fundamentally incompatible theories, the search for the Theory of Everything has proven to be extremely difficult.

Necessitive science makes important contributions to the Theory of Everything, and it also leads the way to finding the "Theory of Everything Relevant." The Theory of Everything Relevant is a theory that defines the actions that are relevant to human survival of the universe (i.e. the actions that are do or die for the world). Ultimate World Theory is this Theory of Everything Relevant.

Since there are limited resources available to search for the descriptive Theory of Everything and since the necessitive Ultimate World Theory directly addresses the efficient use of resources, priority should be given to the development of the Theory of Everything Relevant (i.e. Ultimate World Theory). Moreover, Ultimate World Theory directly addresses the human survival problem in a practical manner. If the human species does not survive, the Theory of Everything is pointless.

The Theory of Everything is actually dependent on Ultimate World Theory for the following two reasons at least:

1) the Theory of Everything is dependent on the Basic Scientific Method and the Basic Scientific Method itself is a form of necessitive knowledge; and

2) the Theory of Everything needs improvement from its current state, and Ultimate World Theory facilitates the necessary improvement over time.

ESSENTIAL WORKFORCE

This list of essential jobs was published by the State of California in March of 2020 as the jobs that were to remain in force during the initial expansion phase of the Coronavirus pandemic. All other jobs were deemed non-essential and were to be shut down by law.

Pandemics are a human survival problem and the Coronavirus pandemic, and the world's reaction to it, provide an excellent example of how a human survival problem takes priority in world events.

This list of essential jobs can be expanded by considering other human survival problems such as global warming (both natural and artificial), and space objects such as meteors and asteroids that can harm the earth and the earth's atmosphere upon impact. We can be reasonably certain that humans are eventually going to need to colonize space and this new space life economy will lead to a large number of new essential jobs.

Finally, we can be certain, by means of Ultimate World Theory, that we as a world are going to need to maximize our individual and group problem solving skill over time, and this will lead to new essential jobs in this new specialized problem solving skill development.   Ultimate World Theory provides guidance for all essential jobs in the future.

1. HEALTHCARE / PUBLIC HEALTH

1. Health care providers and caregivers (including physicians, dentists, psychologists, mid-level practitioners, nurses, assistants, and aids; infection control and quality assurance personnel; pharmacists; physical, respiratory, speech and occupational therapists and assistants; social workers and providers serving individuals with disabilities including developmental disabilities; optometrists; speech pathologists; chiropractors; diagnostic and therapeutic technicians; and radiology technologists).

2. Workers required for effective clinical, command, infrastructure, support service, administrative, security and intelligence operations across the direct patient care and full healthcare and public health spectrum, including accounting, administrative, admitting and discharge, engineering, accrediting, certification, licensing, credentialing, epidemiological, source plasma and blood donation, food service, environmental services, housekeeping, medical records, information technology and operational technology, nutritionists, sanitarians; emergency medical services workers; prehospital workers including but not limited to urgent care workers; inpatient and hospital workers; outpatient care workers; home care workers; workers at long-term care facilities, residential and community-based providers; workplace safety workers).

3. Workers needed to support transportation to and from healthcare facilities and provider appointments.

4. Workers needed to provide laundry services, food services, reprocessing of medical equipment, and waste management.

5. Vendors and suppliers (including imaging, pharmacy, oxygen services, durable medical equipment)

6. Workers who perform critical clinical research, development, and testing needed for COVID-19 response.

7. Workers in other medical and life science facilities (including Ambulatory Health and Surgical, Blood Banks, Clinics, Community Mental Health, Comprehensive Outpatient rehabilitation, End Stage Renal Disease, Health Departments, Home Health care, Hospices, Hospitals, Long Term Care, Organ Pharmacies, Procurement Organizations, Psychiatric, Residential, Rural Health Clinics and Federally Qualified Health Centers, and retail facilities specializing in medical goods and supplies, including cannabis).

8. Workers for health manufacturing (including life science companies, and companies that have shifted production to medical supplies), materials and parts suppliers, technicians, logistics and warehouse operators, printers, packagers, and distributors of medical equipment (including those who test and repair), personal protective equipment (PPE), isolation barriers, medical gases, pharmaceuticals (including materials used in radioactive drugs, and cannabis products), dietary supplements, blood and

blood products, vaccines, testing materials, laboratory supplies, cleaning, sanitizing, disinfecting or sterilization supplies, personal hygiene products, and tissue and paper towel products.

9. Public health / community health workers, including those who compile, model, analyze and communicate public health information.

10. Behavioral and mental health workers responsible for coordination, outreach, engagement, and treatment to individuals in need of mental health and/or behavioral services.

11. Donors of blood bone marrow, blood stem cell, or plasma and the workers of the organizations that operate and manage related activities.

12. Workers that manage health plans, billing, and health information.

13. Workers who conduct community-based public health functions, conducting epidemiologic surveillance, compiling, analyzing and communicating public health information.

14. Workers performing IT and cybersecurity functions at healthcare and public health facilities.

15. Workers performing security, incident management, and emergency operations functions at or on behalf of healthcare entities including healthcare coalitions.

16. Pharmacy employees, including workers necessary to maintain uninterrupted prescription filling.

17. Workers in retail facilities specializing in medical goods and supplies.

18. Public health and environmental health workers, including workers specializing in environmental health that focus on implementing environmental controls, sanitary and infection control interventions, healthcare facility safety and emergency preparedness planning, engineered work practices, and developing guidance and protocols for appropriate PPE to prevent COVID-19 disease transmission; Public health/ community health workers (including call center workers) who conduct community- based public health functions, conducting epidemiologic surveillance and compiling, analyzing, and communicating public health information.

19. Mortuary services providers, including workers performing mortuary, funeral, cremation burial, cemetery, and related services, including funeral homes, crematoriums, cemetery workers and coffin makers.

20. Workers who coordinate with other organizations to ensure the proper recovery, handling, identification, transportation, tracking, storage, and disposal of human remains and personal effects; certify cause of death; and facilitate access to behavioral and mental health services to the family members, responders, and survivors of an incident.

21. Workers supporting veterinary hospitals and clinics.

2. EMERGENCY SERVICES SECTOR

1. Public, private, and voluntary personnel (front line and management) in emergency management, law enforcement, fire and rescue services, emergency medical services, corrections, rehabilitation and reentry, search and rescue, hazardous material response, and technicians supporting maritime and aviation emergency response.

2. Public Safety Answering Points and 911 call center employees; personnel involved in access to emergency services including the emergency alert system and wireless emergency alerts.

3. Fusion Center employees

4. Workers who support weather disaster / natural hazard monitoring, response, mitigation, and prevention, including personnel conducting, supporting, or facilitating wildfire mitigation activities

5. Workers – including contracted vendors -- who maintain, manufacture, or supply equipment and services supporting law enforcement, fire, EMS, and and emergency service response operations (including safety equipment, electronic security, and uniforms)

6. Workers responding to abuse and neglect of children, elders and dependent adults.

7. Animal control officers and humane officers

8. Security staff to maintain building access control and physical security measures

9. Workers and contracted vendors who maintain and provide services and supplies to public safety facilities, including emergency communication center, public safety answering points, public safety communications centers, emergency operation centers, fire and emergency medical services stations, police and law enforcement stations and facilities.

3. FOOD AND AGRICULTURE

1. Workers supporting groceries, pharmacies, convenience stores, and other retail that sells food or beverage products, and animal/pet food, retail customer support service, information technology support staff, for online orders, pickup/takeout or delivery.

2. Workers supporting restaurant carry-out and quick serve food operations, including food preparation, carry-out and delivery food employees.

3. Food manufacturer employees and their supplier employees to include those employed in food ingredient production and processing facilities; aquaculture and seafood harvesting facilities; livestock, poultry, seafood slaughter facilities; pet and animal feed processing facilities; human food facilities producing by-products for animal food; beverage production facilities; and the production of food packaging, including recycling operations and processing.

4. Farmers, farm and ranch workers, and agribusiness support services to include those employed in auction and sales; grain and oilseed handling, storage, processing and distribution; animal food, feed, and ingredient production, packaging, and distribution; manufacturing, packaging, and distribution of veterinary drugs; truck delivery and transport.

5. Farmers, farm and ranch workers, support service workers and their supplier employees producing food supply domestically and for export to include those engaged in raising, cultivating, harvesting, packing, storing, or delivering to storage or to market or to a carrier for transportation to market any agricultural or horticultural commodity for human consumption; those engaged in producing and harvesting field crops; cannabis growers; agricultural and commodity inspection; fuel ethanol facilities; storage facilities; biodiesel and renewable diesel facilities; and other agricultural inputs

6. Employees and firms supporting food, feed, and beverage distribution and ingredients used in these products including warehouse workers, vendor-managed inventory controllers, and blockchain managers.

7. Workers supporting the sanitation of all food manufacturing processes and operations from wholesale to retail.

8. Workers supporting the growth and distribution of plants and associated products for home gardens.

9. Workers in cafeterias used to feed workers, particularly worker populations sheltered against COVID-19

10. Workers in animal diagnostic and food testing laboratories

11. Workers essential for assistance programs and government payments

12. Government, private, and non-governmental organizations' workers essential for food assistance programs (including school lunch programs) and government payments.

13. Employees of companies engaged in the production, storage, transport, and distribution of chemicals; medicines, including cannabis; vaccines; and other substances used by the food and agriculture industry, including seeds, pesticides, herbicides, fertilizers, minerals, enrichments, and other agricultural production aids.

14. Animal agriculture workers to include those employed in veterinary health (including those involved in supporting emergency veterinary or livestock services); raising of animals for food; animal production operations; livestock markets; slaughter and packing plants, manufacturers, renderers, and associated regulatory and government workforce.

15. Transportation supporting animal agricultural industries, including movement of animal medical and reproductive supplies and material, animal vaccines, animal drugs, feed ingredients, feed, and bedding, live animals, animal medical materials; transportation of deceased animals for disposal; and associated regulatory and government workforce

16. Workers who support sawmills and the manufacture and distribution of fiber and forest products, including, but not limited to timber, paper, and other wood and fiber products

17. Employees engaged in the manufacture and maintenance of equipment and other infrastructure necessary to agricultural production and distribution

18. Workers at animal care facilities that provide food, shelter, veterinary and/or routine care and other necessities of life for animals.

4. ENERGY

1. Workers supporting the energy sector, regardless of the energy source, segment of the system, or infrastructure the worker is involved in, or who are needed to monitor, operate, engineer, and maintain the reliability, safety, environmental health, physical and cyber security of the energy system, including power generation, transmission and distribution.

2. Workers supporting the energy sector, regardless of the energy source, needed for construction, manufacturing, transportation and logistics, maintenance, and permitting.

3. IT and OT technology for essential energy sector operations including support workers, customer service operations, call centers, and emergency response and customer emergency operations; energy management systems, control systems, Supervisory Control and Data Acquisition SCADA systems, and energy sector entity data centers; cybersecurity engineers; and cybersecurity risk management.

4. Workers providing services related to energy sector fuels and supply chains, supporting the procurement, mining, drilling, processing, refining, manufacturing, refueling, construction, logistics, transportation (including marine transport, terminals, rail and vehicle transport), permitting operation and maintenance, security, waste disposal, storage, and monitoring of support for resources;

5. Workers supporting environmental remediation and monitoring.

6. Workers supporting manufacturing and distribution of equipment, supplies, and parts necessary to maintain production, maintenance, restoration, and service at energy sector facilities across all energy sectors, and regardless of the energy source.

7. Workers at Independent System Operators and Regional Transmission Organizations, and Network Operations staff, engineers and technicians to manage the network or operate facilities.

8. Workers at Reliability Coordinator, Balancing Authorities, and primary and backup Control Centers, including but not limited to independent system operators, regional transmission organizations, and balancing authorities; and workers involved in energy commodity trading and scheduling.

9. Mutual assistance personnel, which may include workers from outside of the state or local jurisdiction

10. Retail fuel centers such as gas stations and truck stops, and the distribution systems that support them.

5. WATER AND WASTEWATER

Employees needed to operate and maintain drinking water and wastewater/drainage infrastructure, including:

1. Operational staff at water authorities

2. Operational staff at community water systems

3. Operational staff at wastewater treatment facilities

4. Workers repairing water and wastewater conveyances and performing required sampling or monitoring

5. Operational staff for water distribution and testing

6. Operational staff at wastewater collection facilities

7. Operational staff and technical support for SCADA Control systems

8. Chemical disinfectant suppliers for water and wastewater and personnel protection

9. Workers that maintain digital systems infrastructure supporting water and wastewater operations

6. TRANSPORTATION AND LOGISTICS

1. Employees supporting or enabling transportation functions, including truck drivers, bus drivers, dispatchers, maintenance and repair technicians, warehouse workers, truck stop and rest area workers, towing and recovery services, roadside assistance workers, intermodal transportation personnel, and workers that maintain and inspect infrastructure

2. Working supporting or providing services that enable logistics operations for essential sectors, wholesale and retail sale, including warehousing, cooling, storing, packaging, and distributing products for wholesale or retail sale or use.

3. Workers supporting maintenance and operation of essential highway infrastructure, including roads, bridges, and tunnels.

4. Workers of firms providing services, supplies, and equipment that enable warehouse and operations, including cooling, storing, packaging, and distributing products for wholesale or retail sale or use.

5. Mass transit workers providing critical transit services and/or performing critical or routine maintenance to mass transit infrastructure or equipment.

6. Employees supporting personal and commercial transportation services, including taxis, bicycle services, Transportation Network Companies, and delivery services including Delivery Network Companies

7. Workers responsible for operating dispatching passenger, commuter and freight trains and maintaining rail infrastructure and equipment

8. Maritime transportation and inland waterway workers – to include maintenance and repair – including port authority and commercial facility personnel, dredgers, port workers, mariners, ship crewmembers, ship pilots and tugboat operators, ship supply, chandler, and equipment operators.

9. Workers who support the operation, inspection, and maintenance of essential dams, locks, and levees.

10. Workers who support the inspection and maintenance of aids to navigation and other government-provided services that ensure continued maritime commerce.

11. Workers supporting transportation of chemicals, hazardous, medical, waste and recyclable materials to support critical sectors and infrastructure.

12. Automotive repair, maintenance, and transportation equipment manufacturing and distribution facilities.

13. Transportation safety inspectors, including hazardous material inspectors and accident investigator inspectors

14. Manufacturers and distributors (to include service centers and related operations) of lighting and communication systems, specialized signage and structural systems, emergency response equipment and support materials, printers, printed materials, packaging materials, pallets, crates, containers, and other supplies needed to support manufacturing, packaging staging and distribution operations

15. Postal, parcel, courier, last-mile delivery, and shipping workers, to include private companies who accept, process, transport, and deliver information and goods.

16. Workers who supply equipment and materials for maintenance of transportation equipment.

17. Employees who repair and maintain vehicles, aircraft, rail equipment, marine vessels, bicycles, and the equipment and infrastructure that enables operations that encompass movement of cargo and passengers

18. Workers who support air transportation for cargo and passengers, including operation distribution, maintenance, and sanitation. This includes air traffic controllers, flight dispatchers, maintenance personnel, ramp workers, fueling agents, flight crews, airport safety inspectors and engineers, airport operations personnel, aviation and aerospace safety workers, security, commercial space personnel, operations personnel, accident investigators, flight instructors, and other on- and off-airport facilities workers.

19. Workers critical to the manufacturing, distribution, sales, rental, leasing, repair, and maintenance of vehicles and other transportation equipment (including electric vehicle charging stations) and the supply chains that enable these operations, subject to adhering public health guidance issued by CDPH.

20. Workers who support the operation, inspection, and maintenance of essential public works facilities and operations, including bridges, water and sewer main breaks, fleet maintenance personnel, construction of critical or strategic infrastructure, construction material, suppliers, traffic signal maintenance, emergency location services for buried utilities, maintenance of digital systems infrastructure supporting public works operations, and other emergent issues

21. Workers who support, such as road and line clearing, to ensure the availability of needed facilities, transportation, energy and communications.

7. COMMUNICATIONS AND INFORMATION TECHNOLOGY

1. Maintenance of communications infrastructure- including privately owned and maintained communication systems- supported by technicians, operators, call-centers, wireline and wireless providers, cable service providers, satellite operations, Internet Exchange Points, Network Access Points, back haul and front haul facilities, and man-ufacturers and distributors of communications equipment.
2. Workers performing functions related to undersea cable infrastructure and support facilities, including cable landing sites, beach manhole vaults and covers, submarine cable depots, and submarine cable ship facilities
3. Government and private sector employees supporting Department of Defense inter-net and communications facilities.
4. Workers who support radio, television, and media service, including, but not limited to front line news reporters, studio, and technicians for newsgathering, reporting, and publishing news.
5. Network Operations staff, engineers and/or technicians to include IT managers and staff, HVAC & electrical engineers, security personnel, software and hardware engi-neers, and database administrators that manage the network or operate facilities
6. Workers responsible for infrastructure construction and restoration, including con-tractors for construction and engineering of fiber optic cables, buried conduit, small cells, other wireless facilities, and other communications sector-related infrastructure. This includes construction of new facilities and deployment of new technology re-quired to address congestion or customer usage on remote services.
7. Installation, maintenance and repair technicians that establish, support or repair ser-vice as needed.
8. Central office personnel to maintain and operate central office, data centers, and other network office facilities, and critical support personnel assisting front line em-ployees
9. Customer service and support staff, including managed and professional services as well as remote providers of support to transitioning employees to set up and maintain home offices, who interface with customers to manage or support service environments and security issues, including payroll, billing, fraud, logistics and troubleshooting
10. Workers providing electronic security, fire, monitoring, and life safety services, and who ensure physical security, cleanliness, and the safety of facilities and personnel, including those who provide temporary licensing waivers for security personnel to work in other States or Municipalities.
11. Dispatchers involved with service repair and restoration
12. Retail customer service personnel at critical service center locations for onboarding customers, distributing and repairing equipment and other supply chain personnel, to support individuals' remote emergency communications needs;
13. External Affairs personnel to assist in coordinating with local, state, and federal officials to address communications needs supporting COVID-19 response, public safety, and national security.
14. Workers responsible for ensuring that persons with disabilities have access to and the benefits of various communications platforms, including those involved in the pro-vision of telecommunication relay services, closed captioning of broadcast television

for the deaf, video relay services for deaf citizens who prefer communication via American Sign Language over text, and audio-description for television programming.

15. Workers who support command centers, including, but not limited to Network Operations Command Centers, Broadcast Operations Control Center and Security Operations Command Centers

16. Data center operators, including system administrators, HVAC & electrical engineers, security personnel, IT managers and purchasers, data transfer solutions engineers, software and hardware engineers, and database administrators

17. Workers who support client service centers, field engineers, and other workers supporting critical infrastructure, as well as manufacturers and supply chain vendors that provide hardware and software, support services, research and development, information technology equipment (to include microelectronics and semiconductors), and HVAC and electrical equipment for critical infrastructure and test labs and certification agencies that qualify such equipment for critical infrastructure.

18. Workers needed to pre-empt and respond to cyber incidents involving critical infrastructure,, and entities supporting the functioning of critical infrastructure sectors

19. Suppliers, designers, transporters and other workers supporting the manufacture, distribution, and construction of essential global, national and local infrastructure for computing services (including cloud computing services and teleworking capabilities), business infrastructure, financial transactions, web-based services, and critical manufacturing.

20. Workers supporting communications systems, information technology, and work from home solutions

21. Employees required to support Software as a Service businesses that enable remote working, performance of business operations, distance learning, media services, and digital health offerings, or required for technical support crucial for business continuity and connectivity.

8. GOVERNMENT OPERATIONS AND OTHER COMMUNITY-BASED ESSENTIAL FUNCTIONS

1. Critical government workers, as defined by the employer and consistent with Continuity of Operations Plans and Continuity of Government plans.

2. County workers responsible for determining eligibility for safety net benefits

3. The Courts, consistent with guidance released by the California Chief Justice

4. Workers who support administration and delivery of unemployment insurance programs, income maintenance, employment service, disaster assistance, workers' compensation insurance and benefits programs, and pandemic assistance

5. Workers to ensure continuity of building functions, including but not limited to security and environmental controls, the manufacturing and distribution of the products required for these functions, and the permits and inspection for construction.

6. Elections personnel

7. Federal, State, and Local, Tribal, and Territorial employees who support Mission Essential Functions and communications networks

8. Trade Officials (FTA negotiators; international data flow administrators)

9. Weather forecasters

10. Workers that maintain digital systems infrastructure supporting other critical government operations

11. Workers who support necessary credentialing, vetting and licensing operations for critical sector workers and operations.

12. Workers who are critical to facilitating trade in support of the national, state, and local emergency response supply chain

13. Workers supporting public and private childcare establishments, pre-K establishments, K-12 schools, colleges, and universities for purposes of distance learning, provision of school meals, or care and supervision of minors to support essential workforce across all sectors

14. Staff at government offices who perform title search, notary, and recoding services in support of mortgage and real estate services and transactions;

15. Workers and instructors supporting academies and training facilities and courses for the purpose of graduating students and cadets that comprise the essential workforce for all identified critical sectors

16. Clergy for essential support and faith-based services that are provided through streaming or other technologies that support physical distancing and state public health guidelines.

17. Human services providers, especially for at risk populations, including home delivered meal providers for older adults, people with disabilities, and others with chronic health conditions; home-maker services for frail, homebound, older adults; personal assistance services providers to support activities of daily living for older adults, people with disabilities, and others with chronic health conditions who live independently in the community with supports and services; home health providers who deliver health care services for older adults, people with disabilities, and others with chronic health conditions who live independently in the community with supports and services.

18. Government entities, and contractors that work in support of local, state, and federal public health and medical mission sets, including but not limited to supporting access to healthcare and associated payment functions, conducting public health functions, providing medical care, supporting emergency management, or other services necessary for supporting the COVID-19 response.

9. CRITICAL MANUFACTURING

1. Workers necessary for the manufacturing of metals, industrial minerals, semiconductors, materials and products needed for supply chains of the critical infrastructure sectors.

2. Workers necessary for the manufacturing of materials and products needed to manufacture medical equipment and personal protective equipment

3. Workers necessary for mining and production of critical minerals, materials and associated essential supply chains, and workers engaged in the manufacture and maintenance of equipment and other infrastructure necessary for mining production and distribution.

4. Workers who produce or manufacture parts or equipment that supports continued operations for any essential services and increase in remote workforce, including computing and communication devices, semiconductors, and equipment such as security tools for Security Operations Centers (SOCs) or data centers.

5. Workers manufacturing or providing parts and equipment that enable the maintenance and continued operation of essential businesses and facilities.

10. FINANCIAL SERVICES

1. Workers who are needed to process and maintain systems for processing financial transactions and services, including payment, clearing, and settlement; wholesale funding; insurance services; and capital markets activities
2. Workers who are needed to maintain orderly market operations to ensure the continuity of financial transactions and services.
3. Workers who are needed to provide business, commercial, and consumer access to banking and non-bank financial and lending services, including ATMs, lending money transmission, and to move currency, checks, securities, and payments
4. Workers who support financial operations, such as those staffing call, data and security operations centers, managing physical security, or providing accounting services.
5. Workers supporting production and distribution of debit and credit cards.
6. Workers providing electronic point of sale support personnel for essential businesses and workers.

11. CHEMICAL & HAZARDOUS MATERIALS

1. Workers supporting the chemical and industrial gas supply chains, including workers at chemical manufacturing plants, workers in laboratories, workers at distribution facilities, workers who transport basic raw chemical materials to the producers of industrial and consumer goods, including hand sanitizers, food and food additives, pharmaceuticals, textiles, building materials, plumbing, electrical and paper products.
2. Workers supporting the safe transportation of chemicals, including those supporting tank truck cleaning facilities and workers who manufacture packaging items
3. Workers supporting the production of protective cleaning and medical solutions, personal protective equipment, disinfectants, and packaging that prevents the contamination of food, water, medicine, among others essential products
4. Workers supporting the operation and maintenance of facilities (particularly those with high risk chemicals and/ or sites that cannot be shut down) whose work cannot be done remotely and requires the presence of highly trained personnel to ensure safe operations, including plant contract workers who provide inspections
5. Workers who support the production and transportation of chlorine and alkali manufacturing, single-use plastics, and packaging that prevents the contamination or supports the continued manufacture of food, water, medicine, and other essential products, including glass container manufacturing
6. Workers at nuclear facilities, workers managing medical waste, workers managing waste from pharmaceuticals and medical material production, and workers at laboratories processing test kits
7. Workers who support hazardous materials response and cleanup
8. Workers who maintain digital systems infrastructure supporting hazardous materials management operations
9. Workers who support the removal, storage, and disposal of residential and commercial solid waste and hazardous waste, including landfill and recycling operations.

12. DEFENSE INDUSTRIAL BASE

1. Workers who support the essential services required to meet national security commitments to the federal government and U.S. Military, including, but are not limited to, space and aerospace workers, nuclear matters workers, mechanical and software engineers (various disciplines), manufacturing and production workers, IT support, security staff, security personnel, intelligence support, aircraft and weapon system mechanics and maintainers, and sanitary workers who maintain the hygienic viability of necessary facilities.

2. Personnel working for companies, and their subcontractors, who perform under contract or sub-contract to the Department of Defense (DoD) and the Department of Energy (DoE) (on nuclear matters), as well as personnel at government-owned/contractor operated facilities, and who provide materials and services to the DoD and DoE (on nuclear matters), including support for weapon systems, software systems and cybersecurity, defense and intelligence communications, surveillance, sale of U.S. defense articles and services for export to foreign allies and partners (as authorized by the U.S. government), and space systems and other activities in support of our military, intelligence, and space forces.

13. INDUSTRIAL, COMMERCIAL, RESIDENTIAL, and SHELTERING FACILITIES AND SERVICES

1. Construction Workers who support the construction, operation, inspection, and maintenance of construction sites and construction projects (including housing, commercial, and mixed-use construction); and workers who support the supply chain of building materials from production through application/installation, including cabinetry, fixtures, doors, cement, hardware, plumbing, electrical, heating/cooling, refrigeration, appliances, paint/coatings, and employees who provide services that enable repair materials and equipment for essential functions.

2. Workers such as plumbers, electricians, exterminators, and other service providers who provide services that are necessary to maintaining the safety, sanitation, construction material sources, and essential operation of construction sites and construction projects (including those that support such projects to ensure the availability of needed facilities, transportation, energy and communications; and support to ensure the effective removal, storage, recycling and disposal of solid waste and hazardous waste)

3. Workers such as plumbers, electricians, exterminators, and other service providers who provide services that are necessary to maintaining the safety, sanitation, and essential operation of residences, businesses, and buildings such as hospitals and senior living facilities, including any facility supporting COVID-19 response.

4. Workers who support the supply chain of building materials from production through application and installation, including cabinetry, fixtures, doors, cement, hardware, plumbing (including parts and services), electrical, heating and cooling, refrigeration, appliances, paint and coatings, and workers who provide services that enable repair materials and equipment for essential functions.

5. Workers in hardware and building materials stores, consumer electronics, technology and appliances retail, and related merchant retailers, wholesalers and distributors that support essential workforce functions where sales and operations cannot be conducted online

6. Warehouse operators, including vendors and support personnel critical for business continuity (including heating, ventilation, and air conditioning (HVAC) and electrical engineers, security personnel, and janitorial staff), e-commerce or online commerce, and customer service for essential functions.

7. Workers supporting the operations of commercial buildings that are critical to safety, security, and the continuance of essential activities, such as on-site property managers, building engineers, security staff, fire safety directors, janitorial personnel, and service technicians (e.g., mechanical, HVAC, plumbers, electricians, and elevator).

8. Workers supporting ecommerce through distribution, warehouse, call center facilities, and other essential operational support functions that accept, store, and process goods, and that facilitate their transportation and delivery

9. Workers distributing, servicing, repairing, installing residential and commercial HVAC systems, boilers, furnaces and other heating, cooling, refrigeration, and ventilation equipment.

10. Workers managing or servicing hotels or other commercial and residential buildings that are used for COVID-19 mitigation and containment measures, treatment measures, provide accommodation for essential workers, or providing housing solutions, including measures to protect homeless populations.

11. Workers responsible for the leasing of residential and commercial properties to provide individuals and families with ready access to available housing.

12. Residential and commercial real estate workers, limited to scheduled property viewings to a potential buying party. This does not extend to open-house viewings, nor viewings with more than one buying party at a time.

13. Professional services, such as legal or accounting services, when necessary to assist in compliance with legally mandated activities and critical sector services

14. Workers responsible for handling property management, maintenance, and related service calls who can coordinate the response to emergency "at-home" situations requiring immediate attention, as well as facilitate the reception of deliveries, mail, and other necessary services.

15. Workers supporting the entertainment industries, studios, and other related establishments, provided they follow covid-19 public health guidance around physical distancing.

16. Workers that provide or determine eligibility for food, shelter, in-home supportive services, child welfare, adult protective services and social services, and other necessities of life for economically disadvantaged or otherwise needy individuals (including family members)

17. Workers performing services in support of the elderly and disabled populations who coordinate a variety of services, including health care appointments and activities of daily living.

18. Workers who provide support to vulnerable populations to ensure their health and well-being including family care providers.

19. Workers providing dependent care services, particularly those whose services ensure essential workers can continue to work.

20. Workers who support food, shelter, and social services, and other necessities of life for economically disadvantaged or otherwise needy individuals, such as those residing in shelters.

21. Workers in laundromats, laundry services, and dry cleaners.

22. Workers providing disinfection services, for all essential facilities in essential sectors

23. Workers necessary for the installation, maintenance, distribution, and manufacturing of water and space heating equipment and its components.

24. Support required for continuity of services, including commercial disinfectant services, janitorial/cleaning personnel, and support personnel functions that need freedom of movement to access facilities in support of front-line employees.

GLOSSARY

challenge/skill balance: a feeling of confidence and control over a person's ability to succeed. It is also known as the golden rule of Flow theory

control theory: a general theory of feedback systems. The overall theme is the use of feedback to maintain stability in a system over time

control theory framework (CTF): a framework based on the five elements of a control system – reference; controller; input; output; and system

essential workforce: a list of essential jobs that are necessary to solve human survival problems, such as the COVID-19 pandemic

feedback: information about a person's performance of a task, which is used as a basis for improvement

flow theory: a psychological theory of optimal experience. It has three primary conditions: clear goals; clear and immediate feedback on progress; and a challenge/skill balance

future of communication: the communication format of the future is the Ultimate World Experiment step of the Ultimate World Scientific Method

future knowledge: knowledge of the future that provides guidance for improving the present

future person: the person of the future is The Ultimate Person

future world: the world of the future is The Ultimate World

future economy: the economy of the future is the Space Life economy

future of the internet: the internet of the future is Human Survival Problem Solver

future proof: unlikely to become obsolete

getting focused: controlling one's attention so as to maximize performance on the Ultimate Person Action List

getting things done: a time management methodology based on the concept of moving planned tasks and projects out of the mind by recording them externally, and then breaking them down into actionable work items

getting relevant: to the Ultimate Person, relevance means relevance to the human survival problem

happiness/performance link: an approach to performing an action that not only maximizes success, but also maximizes happiness

human extinction: the complete end of the human species

human survival problem: the set of natural and artificial threats to the survival of the human species

human survival solution: a list of actions necessary to solve a human survival problem

human survival problem solver (HSPS): a world-wide computer based solutions manager for managing all human survival problems in all safe locations of the universe and all time. It is also known as the future of the internet.

maximum happiness: an on-going, optimal emotional state of mind

maximum problem solving skill over time (MPSSOT): the skill of mastering problem solving with continuous improvement over time

maximum success: on-going successful performance of a person's tasks and projects

personal problem solving skill: a problem solving skill based on applying MPSSOT to personal issues such as health, finances and family

problem: a threat to the achievement of a goal

professional problem solving skill: a problem solving skill based on applying MPSSOT to your occupation

simple solution to all the world's problems: simply teach everyone in the world one new skill, namely, the skill of MPSSOT

solution: a list of actions necessary to solve a problem

system: a generic term for an entity that takes inputs, process them in some fashion, and produces outputs

ultimate group problem solving: a scenario where everyone in the world uses MPSSOT and works together as a problem solving team to solve the human survival problem

ultimate individual problem solving: a scenario where an individual uses MPSSOT to solve both personal and professional problems

ultimate life: a list of seven benefits that are obtained by being an ultimate person

ultimate person (UP): a person who maximizes problem solving skill over time.

ultimate person action list: a list of tasks and projects for managing an ultimate person's actions on a daily basis

ultimate person action list document: a four page document that functions as a control panel for an ultimate person's tasks and projects

ultimate person performance process (UPPP): an ongoing six-step process for maximizing both action performance results and emotional experience (happiness). It adheres to a set of performance rules based on Flow theory.

ultimate person performance rules: a set of action performance rules for maximizing results on the "Step 4 Perform Actions" of the UPPP

ultimate science: the science of the Ultimate World. It is centered around Ultimate World Theory and is put into practice by means of the Ultimate World scientific method. It is also known as the science of "do or die" at the world level. The science of the Ultimate Person is defined within the context of Ultimate World science

ultimate world (UW): a world-wide group of Ultimate People who work together as a team to maximize group problem solving skill over time

ultimate world theory: a scientific theory that specifies the actions necessary to solve all the world's problems, including the human survival problem

UP$_{MAX}$: the maximum number of Ultimate People. UP$_{MAX}$ is the key element in the Supreme Hypothesis of Ultimate World Theory (in short form: UW = UP$_{MAX}$)

ultimate problem: the human survival problem

SAMPLE CERTIFICATES

There are two certificates available to students at www.ultimateperson.com. The first certificate is a beginner certificate that certifies students as a Certified Ultimate Person. The beginner course and certificate are available free of charge.

The second certificate is an expert certificate that certifies students as a Certified Ultimate Person Expert. The expert course and certificate are available through membership in the Ultimate World Membership program.

Ultimate Person Certificate

The Ultimate Person Certificate is awarded to students who successfully complete the Ultimate Person online course at www.ultimateperson.com.

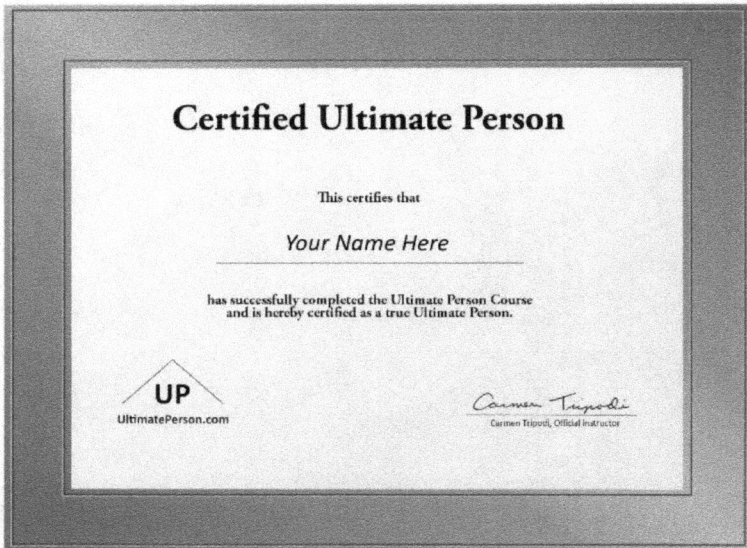

Certified Ultimate Person

This certifies that

Your Name Here

has successfully completed the Ultimate Person Course
and is hereby certified as a true Ultimate Person.

UP
UltimatePerson.com

Carmen Tripodi, Official Instructor

Ultimate Person Expert Certificate

The Ultimate Person Expert Certificate is awarded to students who successfully complete the Ultimate World online course at www.ultimateperson.com.

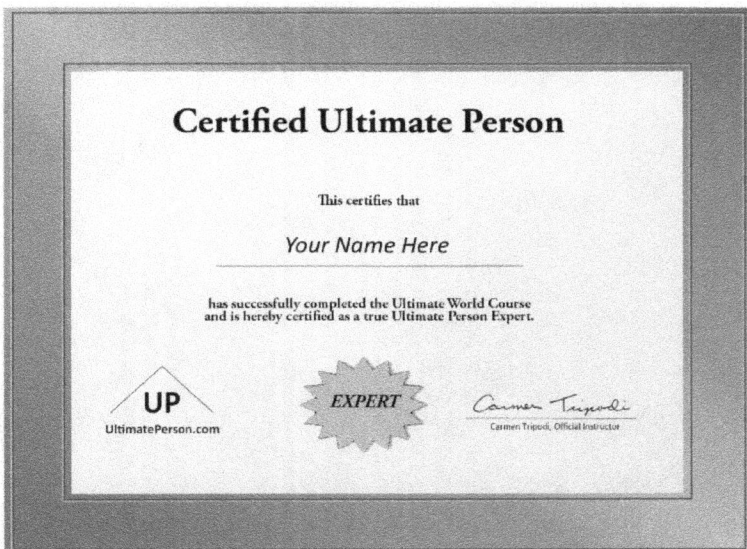

ABOUT THE AUTHOR

Carmen Tripodi is the ultimate authority on the ultimate topics. The two ultimate topics are The Ultimate Person and The Ultimate World. His credibility as an ultimate authority is established by his accurate and reliable definitions of each of these two ultimate topics. His definitions are accurate and reliable, and therefore correct, because they are based on science.

These definitions are detailed in Carmen's two companion books entitled *The Ultimate Person* and *The Ultimate World*.

Now that the scientific definitions of The Ultimate Person and The Ultimate World are available, everyone can now take the steps to become a true Ultimate Person, and The Ultimate World can now be realized. Above all, all the world's problems can now be solved.

Carmen teaches two online courses at www.ultimateperson.com. The first course is a free beginner course that teaches the ultimate skill of "maximum problem solving skill over time," and certifies people as an Ultimate Person. The first course actually implements the simple solution to all the world's problems, free of charge to the world. The second course is an advanced course that teaches the underlying science of The Ultimate Person and The Ultimate World, and certifies students as an expert on these ultimate topics.

His primary contribution to science is the development of Ultimate World Theory, the scientific theory that saves the world. Ultimate World Theory, along with many other scientific innovations, is detailed in *The Ultimate World*.

He also invented (patent pending) the Human Survival Problem Solver, which is also known as the future of the internet. The Human Survival Problem Solver will play an essential role in The Ultimate World, much in the same way the present day internet plays an essential role in the present day world.

Education

Carmen has a Master of Science degree in Computer Information Systems from Claremont Graduate University, and a

Bachelor of Science degree in Electrical Engineering from Pennsylvania State University. He has also taken enough Psychology courses, at both the graduate and undergraduate levels, to informally qualify as having a minor in Psychology.